D1537909

ZOE
SALDANA

BY PETE DELMAR

CAPSTONE PRESS
a capstone imprint

Edge Books are published by Capstone Press,
1710 Roe Crest Drive, North Mankato, Minnesota 56003
www.mycapstone.com

Library of Congress Cataloging-in-Publication Data
Names: Delmar, Pete.
Title: Zoe Saldana / by Pete Delmar.
Description: North Mankato, Minn. : Capstone Press, 2017. | Series: Edge
   books: Hollywood action heroes | Includes bibliographical references and
   index.
Identifiers: LCCN 2016004946| ISBN 9781515709626 (library binding) | ISBN
   9781515712770 (ebook)
Subjects: LCSH: Saldana, Zoe, 1978—Juvenile literature. | Actors--United
   States—Biography—Juvenile literature. | Dancers—United
   States—Biography—Juvenile literature.
Classification: LCC PN2287.S255 D45 2017 | DDC 791.4302/8092—dc23
LC record available at http://lccn.loc.gov/2016004946

Editorial Credits
Linda Staniford, editor; Kyle Grenz, designer;
Eric Gohl, media researcher; Gene Bentdahl, production specialist

Photo Credits
Alamy: AF Archive, 11, 14, 23, Moviestore Collection Ltd, 5, 18, Photos 12, 24;
iStockphoto: gmueses, 8-9; Newscom: Album/Columbia Pictures, 16, Sipa Press/
McMullan/Branch/Patrick McMullan Co., 7, Warner Digital Press Photos, 12,
ZUMA Press/Face to Face, 20-21, 26; Shutterstock: Helga Esteb, 28, Joe Seer, 29,
Tinseltown, cover, 1

Design Elements: Shutterstock

Printed in China.
042016   007737

TABLE OF CONTENTS

Chapter 1

Starting Out

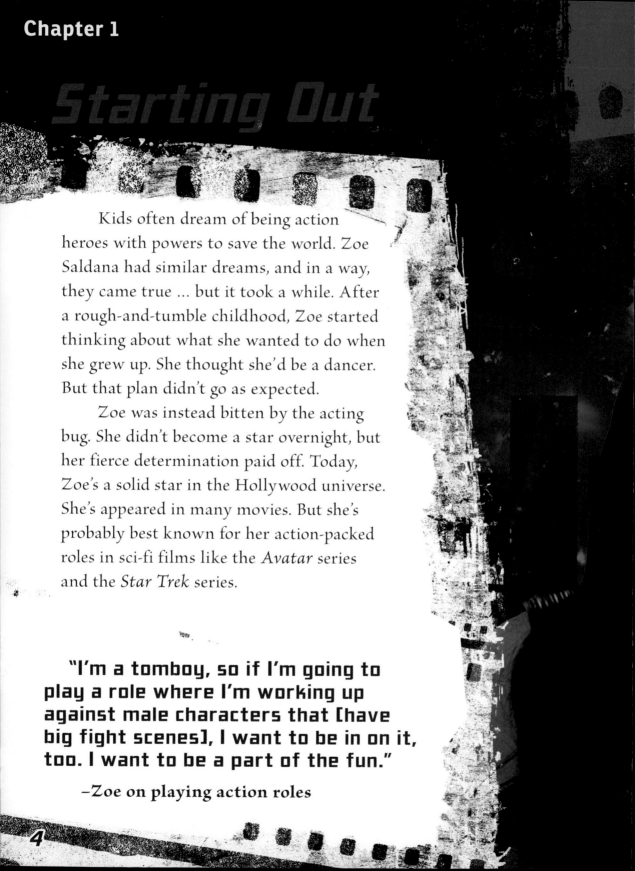

Kids often dream of being action heroes with powers to save the world. Zoe Saldana had similar dreams, and in a way, they came true ... but it took a while. After a rough-and-tumble childhood, Zoe started thinking about what she wanted to do when she grew up. She thought she'd be a dancer. But that plan didn't go as expected.

Zoe was instead bitten by the acting bug. She didn't become a star overnight, but her fierce determination paid off. Today, Zoe's a solid star in the Hollywood universe. She's appeared in many movies. But she's probably best known for her action-packed roles in sci-fi films like the *Avatar* series and the *Star Trek* series.

> **"I'm a tomboy, so if I'm going to play a role where I'm working up against male characters that [have big fight scenes], I want to be in on it, too. I want to be a part of the fun."**
>
> –Zoe on playing action roles

Fast Fact

Zoe did her own stunts for Gamora's big sword fight against her super-villainous sister Nebula.

In 2014 Zoe again played an **extraterrestrial** action hero in *Guardians of the Galaxy*. As the gorgeous green Gamora, she was part of a strange team that fought to save the universe. Zoe Saldana has definitely come a long way from her roots.

extraterrestrial—a life form that comes from outer space; extraterrestrial means "outside of Earth"

Zoe as Gamora in *Guardians of the Galaxy*

Glimpsing a Dream

Zoe Yadira Saldana Nazario was born on June 19, 1978, in Passaic, New Jersey. Her mom, Asalia Nazario, came from Puerto Rico. Her dad, Aridio Saldana, was from the Dominican Republic. Zoe is a second child, between sisters Cisely and Mariel. She also has a half-brother, Nipo.

Zoe's family was living in Queens, New York, when tragedy struck. In 1988 her dad was killed in a car accident. It shattered her world and changed everything. Their mom sent the three girls to live with their grandparents in the Dominican Republic, in the Caribbean. Asalia remained in New York, where she worked hard to pay for her daughters' private school tuition.

"I was never raised to please others. It's not that I'm rebellious, it's just a natural way of being."

–Zoe on growing up

Zoe has a close relationship with her family. Here she is with her two sisters, Mariel (left), Cisely (right), and their mother Asalia (center right).

It was a sad time. But in the Dominican Republic Zoe discovered a strong interest in dance. She enrolled in the highly respected ECOS Espacio de Danza Academy in Santo Domingo. As she trained in dance, Zoe's natural energy and enthusiasm came rushing back. She thought she had found her calling and dreamed of being a professional dancer. However, another destiny was waiting for her.

Chapter 2

Early Ambitions

As a student at Espacio de Danza, Zoe studied modern Latin dance, jazz dance, and ballet. Her first love was ballet. She imagined herself as a **prima ballerina**, the center of attention onstage. Unfortunately, Zoe's training showed that she wasn't good enough to be in the ballet spotlight. But Zoe had "way too much pride and ambition to just be in the **corps**," she later told an interviewer. So her attention turned to other ways to express her talents.

"Ballet taught me to be focused internally on myself, and I think that's why I've been able to succeed in Hollywood in terms of keeping a healthy mental state."
—Zoe on how ballet helped her succeed

This is Santo Domingo in the Dominican Republic, where Zoe studied dance.

At age 17 Zoe found a new passion after returning to the United States. While living in New York, Zoe developed a strong interest in acting. She started taking acting classes after school. Before long she was performing with a theater group called Faces. In their **improv** skits, the group aimed to send positive and uplifting messages to young people like themselves. Zoe also performed with the New York Youth Theater.

prima ballerina—the main female dancer in a ballet company

corps—a group of people working together as part of an acting or dance team

improv—short for improvisation, acting without preparation or rehearsal

First Chances

The New York Youth Theater gave Zoe a chance to experience traditional theater. She appeared in productions of well-known plays such as the musical *Joseph and the Amazing Technicolor Dream Coat*. She was only part of the chorus in that play, but it was enough. Zoe earned a lot of positive attention. Most importantly, she landed a **talent agent**.

Young, ambitious, and beautiful, Zoe was anxious to break into TV and movies. In 1999 she got her first chance. She won small parts in two episodes of the TV drama *Law & Order*. The next year a bigger opportunity came her way. With her background in dance, she was cast in the movie *Center Stage*. It was a natural fit for her. She played Eva Rodriguez, an outspoken ballerina training at the fictional American Ballet Academy. In *Center Stage* Zoe was part of an **ensemble** cast. But she was headed for starring roles.

talent agent—someone who helps actors find work

ensemble—a group of actors who perform together

Most of the cast of *Center Stage* had professional ballet training, like Zoe (who is seen on the left in this picture).

Gaining Experience

Over the next two years Zoe appeared in three more movies. In 2001 she was cast in *Get Over It*, a musical comedy about a high school basketball star. She didn't have a large part, but it was a solid step toward her goal. The following year she starred in *Drumline*. She played the part of a college dance major and love interest of the leading man.

Zoe's ethnic background is a mixture of different groups. Puerto Ricans, like her mom, descend from Africans, Taino Indians, and Europeans, or a combination of these. People from the Dominican Republic, like her dad, are mostly descended from Africans, as well as from the Carib Indians. But Zoe herself identifies as a black woman. She says, "I will honor and respect my black community because that's who I am."

In 2002 Zoe also appeared in her biggest Hollywood production yet. In *Crossroads*, starring Britney Spears, Zoe played one of the lead characters. The movie wasn't a critical hit, but audiences loved it. *Crossroads* was especially popular in Japan, which helped give Zoe international exposure. Moviegoers around the world began to wonder ... who is this Zoe Saldana?

In *Crossroads*, Zoe played one of three friends who go on a road trip after graduation.

ethnic—related to a group of people and their culture

A Moment of Doubt

Playing a pirate is probably something a lot of kids would jump at. And for the grown-up Zoe, it seemed like a dream come true at the time. In 2003 she was cast in *Pirates of the Caribbean: The Curse of the Black Pearl*. Zoe played a minor role, but she would be appearing in a huge Hollywood action adventure. She would work with three major celebrities: Johnny Depp, Orlando Bloom, and Keira Knightley.

> **"As a woman, I always want to find roles that are empowering to women, not just soccer moms, or girlfriends or victims."**
>
> –Zoe on choosing movie parts

It should have been a highlight in Zoe's career. But the feisty young actress found the experience insulting. It was so bad that Zoe seriously considered getting out of the movie business. She hated the way the lead actors were treated compared to those in less important roles, like herself. She had no complaints at all about the big stars. She felt respected by them. But Zoe felt that those in charge gave little respect to actors in smaller roles. The inequality of the whole episode made Zoe steaming mad! Fortunately, she wasn't ready to give up on Hollywood yet.

Fast Fact

Zoe has done fight scenes in many different movies. She takes a lot of pride in the lumps and bruises those scenes cause her. "I work really hard," she says, "and those are proof of the blood, sweat, and tears" she puts into her action roles.

Back in the Game

After her unfortunate experience with *Pirates*, Zoe took a hard look at her career. Was acting really what she wanted to do? She decided that it was. Her faith in the movie business soon returned when she got a chance to work with acclaimed director Steven Spielberg. In 2004 he cast Zoe in his film *The Terminal* with Tom Hanks. Zoe again didn't have a starring role, but Spielberg turned out to be her dream director.

Zoe played Theresa in *Guess Who?*

Fast Fact

Zoe received four award nominations for her performance in *Guess Who?* This recognition came from the Black Reel Awards, the Black Movie Awards, the Image Awards, and the Teen Choice Awards.

Zoe was back in the game. She made several movies over the next five years. Her biggest role was as the leading actress in the 2005 comedy *Guess Who?* Loosely based on the old film *Guess Who's Coming to Dinner*, it was about an African American woman who brings her white boyfriend home to meet her disapproving dad. Some movie reviewers didn't like *Guess Who?* But it was number one at the box office on its opening weekend. For Zoe, even bigger things were just over the horizon.

"I wouldn't want it to get too easy, because it takes away the hunger and excitement of getting something. I like having to chase something I really want, because things that fall in your lap are things you take for granted."

–Zoe on getting good movie roles

Chapter 3

A Breakout Year

By 2009 Zoe had appeared in 19 films. But she still wasn't a household name. In April that began to change. The movie *Star Trek* released that month, and Zoe had a starring part in it. It was finally her big break.

The *Star Trek* **franchise** has a huge worldwide fan base. It began as a TV series in 1966. Several movies followed, starring the same actors who had been in the TV series. But the 2009 film gave *Star Trek* a fresh look, with new actors playing the long-beloved characters.

The Road
Almost Not *Taken*

At the time the role of Uhura was offered to her, Zoe was already hard at work on another big sci-fi action movie—*Avatar.* Knowing little about *Star Trek* she wasn't interested at first. But her *Avatar* director, James Cameron, urged her not to turn down such a big opportunity.

Zoe remembers him saying, "You're kidding me! You're not going to do *Star Trek*?! Give me [the director's] number, and I'll call him." The next thing she knew, they'd convinced her to become Uhura. Today Zoe's a big *Star Trek* fan, and loves the original TV series.

Zoe played Nyota Uhura. In the *Star Trek* universe, Uhura comes from the United States of Africa and speaks Swahili. She is also the chief communications officer on the starship *Enterprise*. This role gave millions of *Star Trek* fans the chance to see Zoe in action. It put her squarely in the spotlight—just where she wanted to be.

franchise— a series of films or TV shows that feature the same characters or follow a continuing storyline

iconic—widely viewed as perfectly capturing the meaning or spirit of something or someone

Fast Fact

The role of Uhura in the original TV series was an iconic one. It was one of the first female African American roles in a mainstream TV series. Zoe felt very honored to get some "amazing pointers" from Nichelle Nichols, who played the original Uhura in the TV series and earlier *Star Trek* movies.

A Mega Movie Event

London, December 10, 2009. That night saw the world premiere of a major 3-D movie—*Avatar*. This mega-blockbuster film turned out to be a massive hit around the world. Zoe played the central character Neytiri, a blue-skinned, long-tailed creature in the alien world of Pandora.

The movie used special computer effects to turn the human actors into the alien Na'vi species. It wasn't easy to recognize Zoe as the character Neytiri. But as the love interest of main character Jake Sully, she got major screen time.

Zoe appears with the cast and crew at the US premiere of *Avatar* in Los Angeles.

Avatar was nominated for Best Picture at the 2010 Academy Awards. It didn't win, but it did win three other major awards. The film made more than $2.7 billion worldwide. Zoe herself won five awards for her work. She was part of the biggest Hollywood film ever made. For Zoe, 2009 was the year in which her career soared to a whole new level.

"Even when I'm whining on the set I feel blessed to be doing what I do."

–Zoe on her career

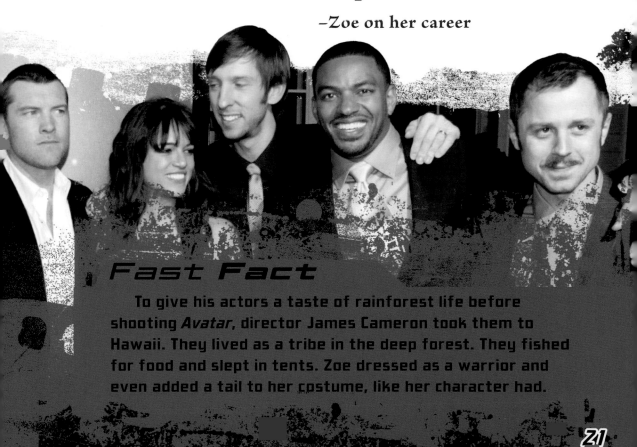

Fast Fact

To give his actors a taste of rainforest life before shooting *Avatar*, director James Cameron took them to Hawaii. They lived as a tribe in the deep forest. They fished for food and slept in tents. Zoe dressed as a warrior and even added a tail to her costume, like her character had.

Chapter 4

Fast Trek To Stardom

With *Star Trek* and *Avatar*, Zoe had earned her place as a genuine blockbuster star. Part of that recognition came from her feisty fight scenes. Zoe takes her physical training seriously. This was especially true when it came to *Avatar*.

The Magic of Avatar

In most animated films, the actors simply read their lines into a microphone. But *Avatar* was different. The actors wore special suits and were wired up electronically. Then they performed action scenes in the studio using a technique called performance capture. Every movement and facial expression they made was fed into a computer. Finally, the actors' images were transformed into the strange and beautiful Na'vi.

Zoe was determined to make her performance perfect. She spent six months preparing to play Neytiri. This included lessons in horseback riding and archery. She also studied martial arts and learned other fighting skills. *Avatar* proved that Zoe could be a powerhouse action star.

"I learn as I go. The moment I get the job, that's when I start doing the research and I end up falling completely in love with the franchise."

–Zoe on preparing for her roles

Zoe's training helped her create Neytiri's grace and agility.

An Actress in Demand

After scoring with *Star Trek* and *Avatar*, Zoe had plenty of roles to choose from. In 2010 she tried her hand at comedy, thrillers, and further action movies. Then in 2011 she got top billing in a dark action-thriller called *Colombiana*. Zoe starred as a stone-cold killer. And although *Colombiana* was a "**B movie**," film reviewers noted Zoe's excellent action-star skills. One even mentioned her top-form "acrobatic" moves.

> "I was super-happy with [*Star Trek Into Darkness*] ... especially knowing science fiction is a genre everyone is keen on watching. Sci-fi is the place for me. I love it."
>
> **–Zoe on her roles in science fiction movies**

In 2012 Zoe took a brief detour away from the action. She starred with Bradley Cooper in *The Words*, a more romantic movie. But Zoe's wise decision to take on *Star Trek* was about to pay off again. The sequel, *Star Trek Into Darkness*, came out in 2013. For Zoe, working with director J.J. Abrams gave her another ideal acting experience. It also gave her a chance to do a little more deep-space bad-guy bashing.

B movie—a low budget movie

Zoe is very happy working on sci-fi movies such as *Star Trek*.

Fast Fact

For her starring role in *Colombiana*, Zoe trained with members of the Los Angeles police. She also did weight training and learned to handle a gun. To top it off she learned an Israeli method of hand-to-hand combat and physical training called Krav Maga.

Deadliest Woman in the Galaxy

By 2014 Zoe had been in several smaller-budget movies as well as a handful of major films. That year she got another chance to show off her action skills. *Guardians of the Galaxy* was based on the Marvel comic book of the same name. In this movie Zoe starred as green-skinned killer Gamora. She's a deep space criminal who joins a bunch of misfits to save the universe. In the process they become heroes.

Fast Fact

Zoe claimed that she and Dave Bautista, who played Drax the Destroyer, were the stunt doubles' "nightmare." They were so good at doing their action scenes that the doubles got fewer hours of work themselves.

Action scenes seem to bring out Zoe's most feisty and fiery self. All the *Guardians* actors wore protective padding when filming fight scenes. But one day Chris Pratt, who plays Star-Lord, forgot his gear in a scene with Gamora. Not knowing this, Zoe kicked Chris so hard he ended up with bruised ribs. Maybe that's why Gamora has been called "the deadliest woman in the galaxy."

Guardians of the Galaxy wasn't just about the action. It also had some genuinely funny moments. Zoe loved the humor in the script. Audiences loved it too.

"... an anti-hero hero movie ... The characters are misfits—insecure, abandoned, hurt, scared, conniving, but good-hearted people. They become heroes without losing their street cred."

–Zoe on *Guardians of the Galaxy*

All-Around Action

Fans will get to see more of Zoe in the next few years. She is set to star in sequels to *Star Trek*, *Avatar* and *Guardians of the Galaxy*. She'll also appear in the movie version of the graphic novel *I Kill Giants*.

At home Zoe and her Italian artist husband Marco Perego have their hands full too. They welcomed twin sons Cy and Bowie in November 2014. Zoe's definitely got plenty of action in her life!

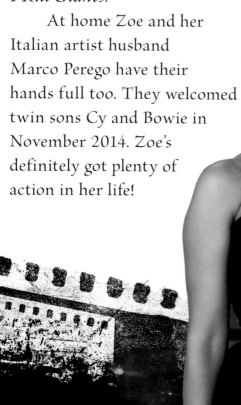

Zoe and Marco are seen here at a charity party for Oscar winners and nominees in 2015.

Fighting for her Cause

Much like her on-screen characters, Zoe doesn't back down from a challenge. She fights fearlessly for what she believes in. Zoe feels it's important to help people less fortunate than herself. After a massive earthquake hit Haiti in 2010, she became involved with the Lend a Hand campaign. This organization helps women living in poverty to provide for themselves and their families. Zoe also works with Brave Beginnings, which provides equipment to help premature babies survive.

Whether battling on strange worlds or helping people in real life, Zoe Saldana always gives it her all. She's an action hero who knows her worth!

"The only thing I want to do and be in life is happy."

–Zoe on what she wants from life

Zoe helps serve Thanksgiving dinner to homeless people at the Los Angeles Mission in 2011.

GLOSSARY

B movie (BEE MOO-vee)—a low budget movie

corps (KOR)—a group of people working together as part of an acting or dance team

ensemble (on-SOM-buhl)—a group of actors who perform together

ethnic (ETH-nik)—related to a group of people and their culture

extraterrestrial (ek-struh-tuh-RESS-tree-uhl)—a life form that comes from outer space; extraterrestrial means "outside of Earth."

franchise (FRAN-chize)—a series of films or TV shows that feature the same characters or follow a continuing storyline

iconic (eye-KON-ik)—widely viewed as perfectly capturing the meaning or spirit of something or someone

improv (IM-prov)—short for improvisation, acting without preparation or rehearsal

prima ballerina (PREE-muh bal-uh-REE-nuh)—the main female dancer in a ballet company

talent agent (TAL-uhnt AY-juhnt)—someone who helps actors find work

READ MORE

Murphy, Maggie. *Zoe Saldana.* Movie Superstars. New York: PowerKids Press, 2011.

Quijano, Jonathan. *Make Your Own Action Thriller.* Make Your Movie. North Mankato, Minn.: Capstone Press, 2012.

Tougas, Joe. *Mind-blowing Movie Stunts.* Wild Stunts. North Mankato, Minn.: Capstone Press, 2016.

INTERNET SITES

FactHound offers a safe, fun way to find Internet sites related to this book. All of the sites on FactHound have been researched by our staff.

Here's all you do:

Visit *www.facthound.com*

Type in this code: 9781515709626

Check out projects, games and lots more at
www.capstonekids.com

INDEX

9246